ABC
BIRDS

AF438668

ABC BIRDS

Learn the alphabet with birds!

P.G. Hibbert

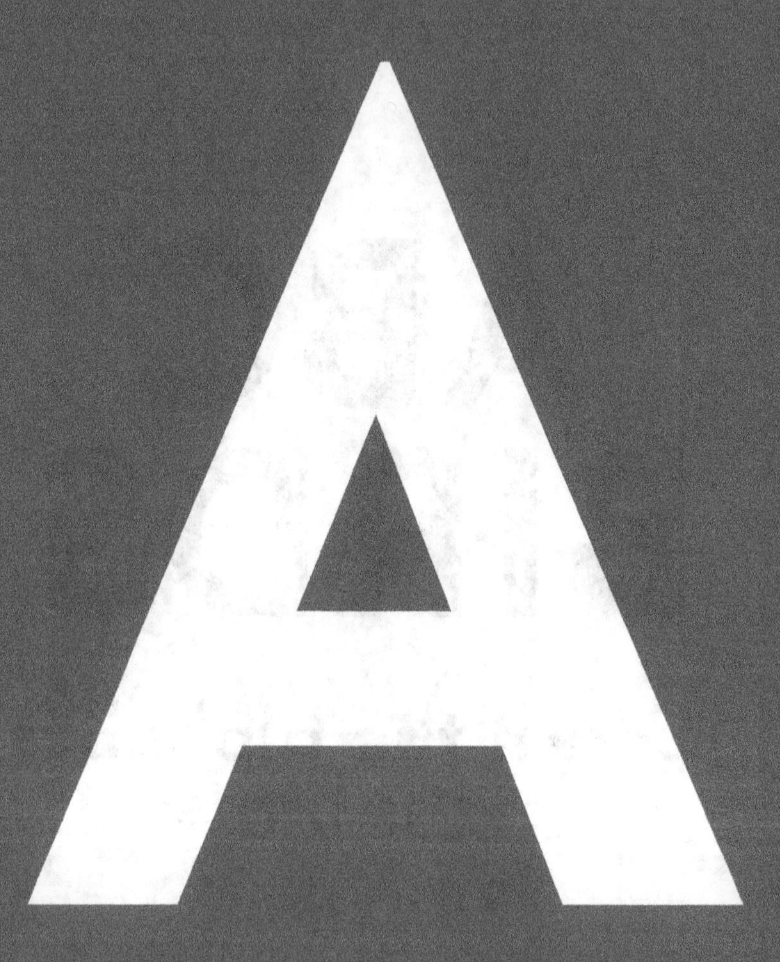
A

American Goldfinch

Baltimore Oriole

Chicken

Duck

Eagle

Flamingo

Goose

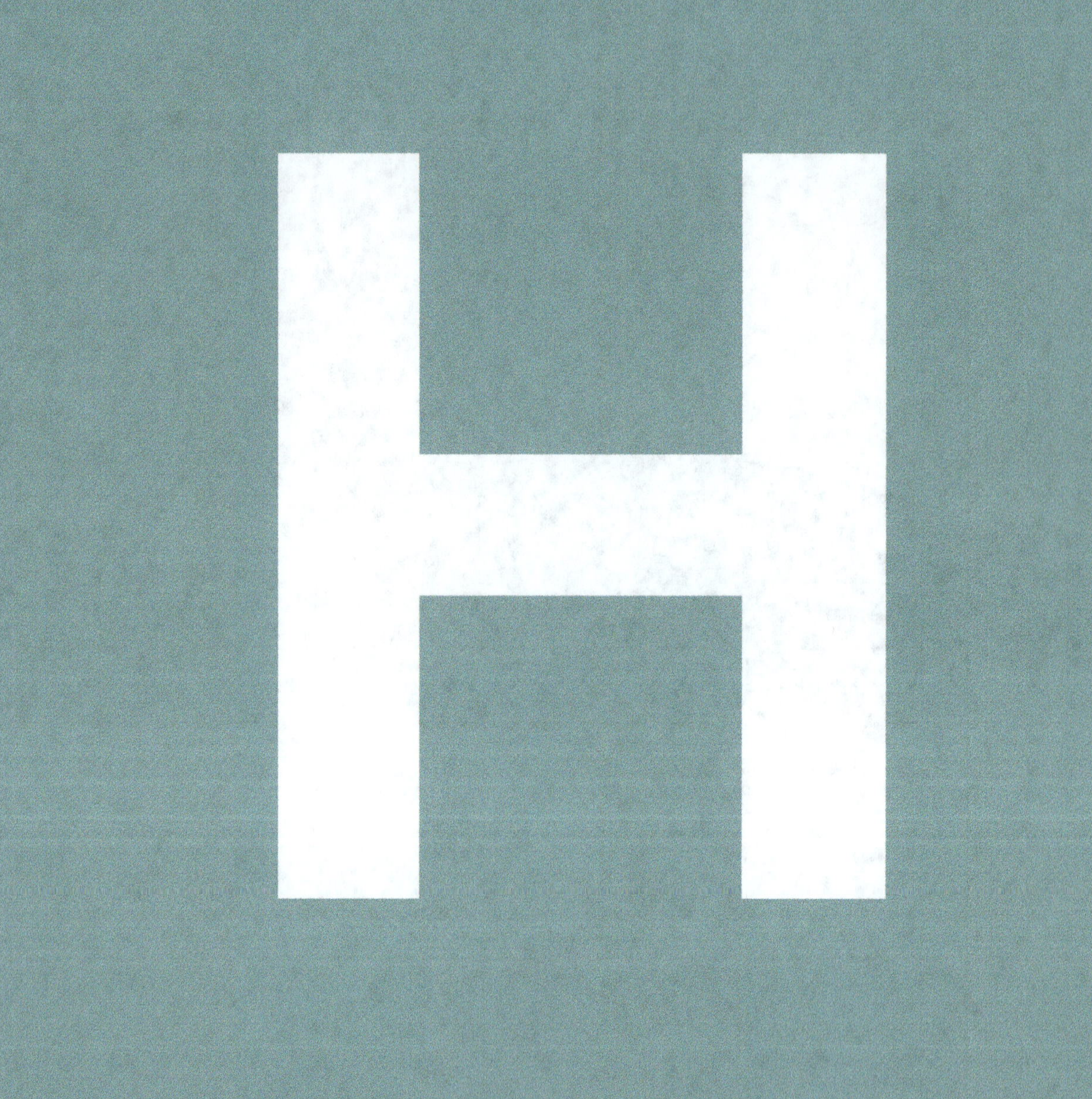

Hawk

Indian Ringneck

Jay

Kiwi

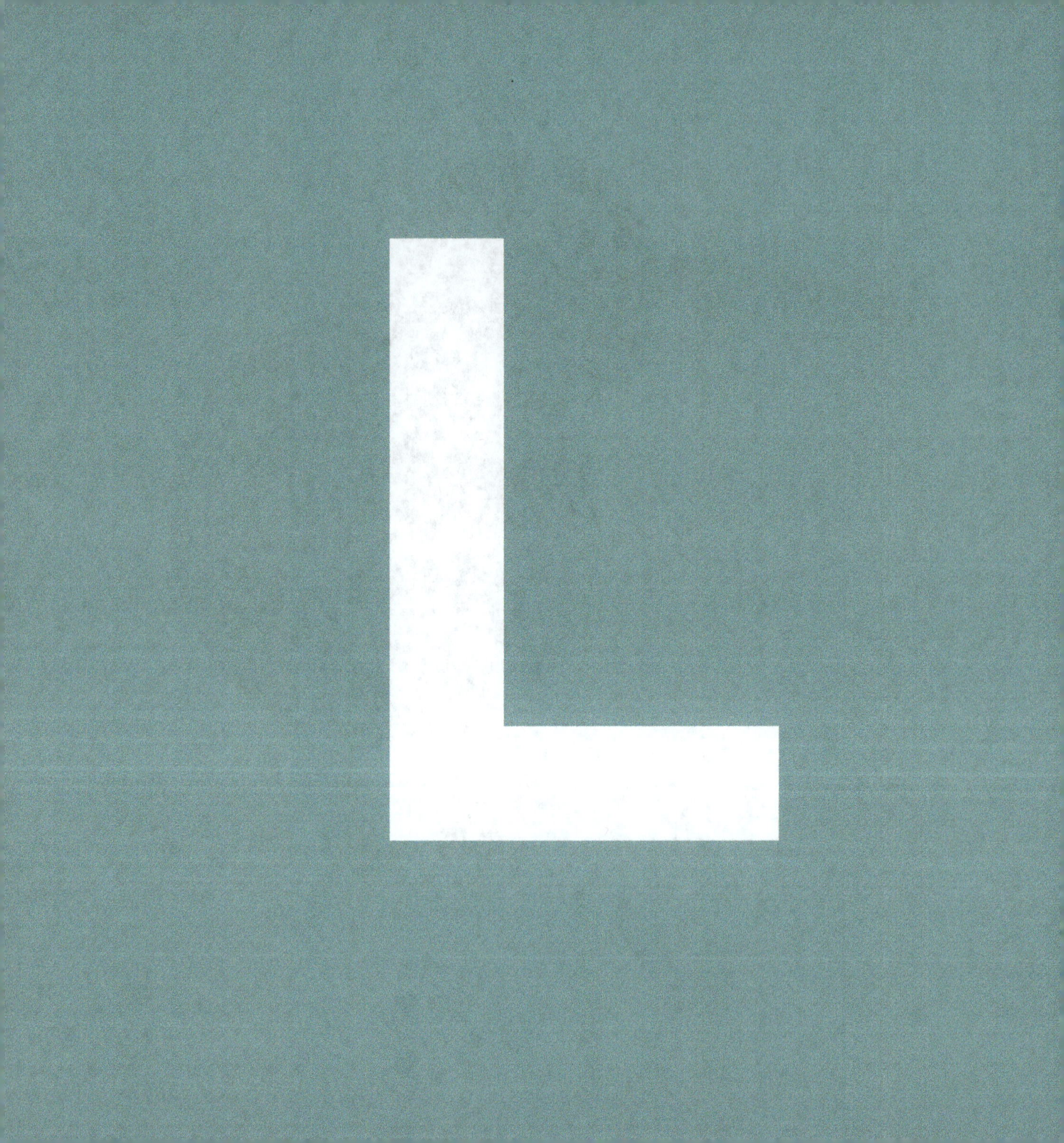

Lark

Magpie

Nightingale

Ostrich

Parrot

Quail

Raven

Sparrow

Toucan

Upland Sandpiper

Vulture

Wild Turkey

Xantu's Hummingbird

Yellow-rumped Seedeater

Zeledon's Antbird